Mindful School.
Mindful Community.

McLEAN SCHOOL'S CURRICULUM
AND GUIDE FOR EDUCATORS

Charleston, SC
www.PalmettoPublishing.com

Mindful School. Mindful Community.
Copyright © 2018 by McLean School

Hardcover ISBN: 978-1-64990-765-3
Paperback ISBN: 978-1-64990-766-0
eBook ISBN: 978-1-64990-767-7

Mindful School.
Mindful Community.

McLEAN SCHOOL'S CURRICULUM
AND GUIDE FOR EDUCATORS

**INFORMATION, RESOURCES, AND MATERIALS
TO DEVELOP, IMPLEMENT, AND SUSTAIN A K-12 MINDFULNESS PROGRAM**

Frankie Engelking, MA
Rosie Waugh, MEd, MS

This book is dedicated to the faculty, staff, students, and parents of McLean School who have embraced mindfulness and continue to share its benefits with others.

Table of Contents

Resources for Heartfulness and Gratitude

Resources for Listening

Resources for Engagement of the Senses

Creating a Personalized Mindfulness Practice

Reference

FOREWORD BY CHRISTINA COSTELO

Program Manager at Mindful Schools

McLean School has compiled a rich series of developmentally appropriate and in-spired activities and resources that help create memorable, experiential practices in mindfulness. This curriculum will help ground fundamental concepts for young people, as well as ignite a curiosity that will help nourish the seeds of mindfulness.

When we first started training the community at McLean School, we were impressed by their dedication to pro-social learning environments, especially in mindfulness.

The school leadership, staff, and parents alike worked together for years slowly building support mechanisms to allow a culture of mindfulness to flourish. Now they've become a beacon of inspiration and learning for other schools trying to implement school-wide mindfulness programming. We at Mindful Schools, are always proud to share their story with others, and continue to actively support their initiatives in mindfulness.

Practicing mindfulness can help facilitate several long-term social, emotional, and even physical benefits. We can remember to take pause, especially during big moments. We can choose our response rather than allowing our habits to react for us. We can feel more connected to one another through developing empathy and gratitude. We can notice our internal experience and understand our needs better. By simply practicing present mo-ment awareness with curiosity and non-judgement, we can begin to attune and let our best selves shine.

How you practice mindfulness is limitless because you can practice it in every moment. The most common and recommended modality for strengthening one's capacity in mindfulness is through mindful meditation. This helps you integrate more mindful mo-ments through the day, according to research. However, when beginning to learn about mindfulness, especially for children, it's important to get creative to help bring the concepts and practices to life. Using relatable metaphors, engaging activities, and fun games connects children to their own innate capacity to practice presence.

It teaches them early on how practicing mindfulness can be integrated into every moment. Allowing them to savor goodness while laughing with a friend, notice and calm erratic nerves before a test, find confidence in their voice before presenting their project, and to act with greater compassion towards themselves and others.

Even if you facilitate these lessons and activities with limited personal experience with mindfulness, you are sure to connect to the practice as well.

With gratitude for your wonderful work and deep impact in your school community (and beyond!), we thank you for this wonderful contribution to this field.

INTRODUCTION

Michael Saxenian, Head of McLean School

Mindfulness and education are a perfect pairing. Jon Kabat-Zinn, a pioneer of the practice, refers to mindfulness as "paying attention on purpose," and at McLean School it's become a powerful tool for settling mind and body in ways that exponentially enhance learning. We have seen – up close and over time – what a mindfulness practice can do for individual students of all ages and for our school as a whole. And in an age of heightened anxiety due to climate change, societal unrest, and the global pandemic, we think it is more important than ever. Spoiler alert: it's transformational.

A scientific and skills-based program, mindfulness taps into thoughts, feelings, and surroundings to calm the nervous system, reduce stress, and increase focus in school and in life. At McLean, it's integrated into all that we do, and mindful practices are a mainstay for students, faculty, and even our families. As with everything, some take to it faster or more fully than others. We developed a thoughtful curriculum with many access points and activities for just this reason, and it's fair to say that everyone at McLean benefits from the program as a result.

Of course, creating a culture of mindfulness doesn't happen overnight. Prior to my arrival at McLean, I had a keen understanding, disconcerting as it was, of the effect of stress on learning. This was thanks in part to clinical neuropsychologist William Stixrud, whose compelling workshops and writing on adolescent brain development helped shape my thinking on the subject. In addition, I had a yoga practice that helped to ground me in my personal life, and as an administrator at a Quaker School I knew the powerful part silence and meditation can play in helping students settle their systems for learning. So when I started as Head of McLean School in 2013, I was thrilled to learn that a few teachers, along with a parent volunteer--a physician--were doing occasional mindfulness lessons in her children's classrooms around the foundational tenets of breathing, body awareness, and gratitude. What could be better? Except, perhaps, making sure all our students have access to these resources. I got to work.

I knew McLean would be a fertile environment for a mindfulness program, with creative teachers dedicated to doing whatever they can to support their students in becoming successful learners and healthy human beings. We incorporated mindfulness education into a new position of Director of Student and Community Wellness, and hired a Mindfulness Program Coordinator. We are fortunate that Frankie Engelking and Rosie Waugh have taken on those roles and run with them. Their passion for the program and their own love of learning have helped us become the leader in mindfulness education we are today. I would like to thank Co-Director of Communications and Marketing, Elizabeth Shannon, and Communications and Marketing Specialist, Robbie Gross, for the countless hours of work in preparing this book for publication.

On the pages that follow, we are pleased to share what we do and how we do it so that other teachers and their students may understand, implement, and grow as a result. A successful mindfulness program takes effort but mindfulness itself is not hard, and the outcomes certainly make a strong case: reduced stress and anxiety, increased focus and self-regulation, improved academic performance, and so much more.

As we tell our students, it's called a practice because you have to practice it. And the more you practice, the easier and more automatic it becomes. Our students are putting their skills to use every day in all sorts of contexts, from the playing field to test preparation. Parents report that mindfulness is having an impact on life at home, and some come to us and ask for training. Prospective hires are drawn to McLean, they tell me, in part for the work we're doing in this area. Recently one of our alumni shared that he introduced mindfulness to his college basketball team, and it became a regular part of their practice routine.

Every day at McLean, I'm reminded that this work is relevant, meaningful, and makes learning – and life – better for our students. Isn't that what teaching is all about?

"Mindfulness is awareness that arises through paying attention, on purpose, in the present moment, non-judgementally,"

Jon Kabat-Zinn

McLean School
Transformative.

How to Use This Curriculum

McLean School is pleased to provide this resource rich with activities and ideas for implementing a successful mindfulness program in your school community. Our curriculum is organized around the five tenets of mindfulness: breathing and body awareness, emotions, heartfulness and gratitude, listening and communication, and engagement of the senses.

Unlike teaching guides specific to subject area or grade level – or both – McLean's mindfulness curriculum is a menu of material that can be easily incorporated into the existing learning environment. At McLean, that's always been our goal: to make mindfulness an integrated, natural part of a student's everyday educational experience. And we believe that this is what differentiates our approach; we have made mindfulness a core part of our school culture, rather than simply a stand-alone program.

As a leader in mindfulness education, we are often approached by other educators asking, "where do we start?" In this book, we aim to capture and consolidate the "how" of what we do in a way that is accessible and applicable to teachers as well as anyone working with kids, including their parents. You'll find practical and playful activities specific to each of the five foundational tenets, and although we've grouped them together by age range, you'll see that many if not most of the skills are variations on a theme (glitter jars, for example, are introduced and reintroduced in subsequent sections). Each tenet can be presented as its own individual lesson or to enhance existing ones.

There is much to say about the science of mindfulness, and while we do touch on it throughout the book, we assume that those reading this curriculum have already come to understand the value of mindfulness and the reasons why it works. With these outcomes in mind, our curriculum provides very doable steps and strategies for creating (or enriching) a mindfulness practice in your school, home, or other setting. Our students are putting their skills to use each and every day: before a big test or pop quiz, in the locker room prior to a game, when having a hard conversation, or in the words of one fourth grader, "just to start the day off right."

May you and the children in your life find the practice as transformational as we have.

TENETS OF MINDFULNESS

Breathing and Body Awareness

Awareness of Emotions

Heartfulness and Gratitude

Listening and Positive Communication

Engagement of the Senses

Breathing and Body Awareness

The foundation of any mindfulness practice is breathing. It's not as easy as it sounds! But with practice, it becomes a valuable tool to focus the mind and still the body.

Diaphragmatic (deep belly) breathing activates the parasympathetic nervous system, which allows the body to slow down and move from an activated "fight or flight" mode into a calmer "rest and restore" state. Allowing more oxygen into the body forces the release of carbon dioxide and other toxins, which settles the system and makes the brain and body available for learning. Mindful breathing – whether during times of meditation or as a tool throughout the day – paves the way for a more mindful response to daily stressors and situations.

Goal of this section: build awareness of breath as a tool for self-regulation.

Awareness of Emotions

When emotions run high, we are prone to conflict and impulsivity. Coming into awareness of what we're feeling is an important first step in changing negative behaviors: "name it to tame it."

Neuroplasticity of the brain allows us to develop manageable responses to highly emotional states. Learning to pause long enough to identify a feeling – the sensation itself, and where in your body you feel it – allows for a more mindful response, increased self-control, and improved interactions. Over time, by practicing emotional awareness in this way, we are able to create new pathways in the brain that lead to more positive, productive behaviors.

Goal of this section: recognize the range of feelings, difficulties, and needs in ourselves and others.

Heartfulness and Gratitude

By nature, human beings are wired to expect the worst – it's a primitive thought pattern once required for survival that doesn't serve us well in this day and age. Focusing on the positive is a powerful factor in emotional and relational well-being; appreciation for self and others increases dopamine levels in the brain – the "feel good" hormones – while decreasing stress hormones like adrenaline and cortisol. Positivity begets positivity: a gratitude practice leads to increased acceptance of ourselves and others, and trains our brains for the better.

Goal of this section: develop an appreciation of the good in our lives.

Listening and Positive Communication

The average person is listening at only 25 percent capacity – most of the time, we're thinking about what we want to say next, or distracted by intrusive, unrelated thoughts. Trying to pay attention when distracted is actually quite stressful and the body reacts accordingly by going into a bit of a panic state, with increased anxiety and blood pressure.

Mindful listening – focusing on words and sounds – brings our awareness to the distractions and reminds us to refocus and listen with intention. Staying present in communication allows us to hear the entirety of what's being said and leads to more authentic connections with others.

Goal of this section: develop awareness of sound and cultivate positive ways to communicate.

Engagement of the Senses

Intentionally focusing on one of the five senses – sight, sound, smell, taste, or touch – quiets the mind and draws attention to what's happening in a given moment. Coupled with mindful breathing, engaging with our senses in this way deepens our connection with the environment and keeps us from getting bogged down in thoughts that can be distracting and anxiety producing. Over time, and with practice, the ability to get out of one's head and into one's body is a calming and quick-acting tool.

Goal of this section: notice and engage the senses to settle body and mind.

Creating a Personalized Mindfulness Practice

Mindfulness is a life skill, and – like anything – there comes a point when young people are encouraged and expected to take responsibility for their own personal practice. The beauty of McLean's mindfulness curriculum is that it is embedded into everyday life, especially in the early grades; for students in the upper grades, we provide individual and group activities and, most importantly, the time and space for students to develop their own practice. Those who work with teens know that sometimes they balk at one more thing to have to think about – so it's important to emphasize that maintaining a mindfulness practice makes life easier, not harder, and encourage them to adapt the skills to meet their own individual needs.

Goal of this section: empower students to develop a personal practice that will help them successfully manage the stresses of daily life.

K - 2

Resources for Breathing and Body Awareness

GOAL OF THIS SECTION: BUILD AWARENESS OF BREATH AS A TOOL FOR SELF-REGULATION.

Hoberman Sphere

Video: Breathing with a Sphere by Elizabeth Miller[1]

Poster, Mindfulness On-the-Go, breathing steps using the road metaphor[2].

Anchor Hand

Ask students to hold up their nondominant hand spreading fingers. Tell them to:

- Use the index finger of the hand you write with.

- Now trace each outspread finger in time with a full cycle of breath.

- Feel your tracing finger move up as you inhale, keep looking as your finger moves down the other side, and you exhale.

- When you get to the end of your hand, your thumb or finger, just reverse and keep on breathing and looking.

Slow Down, Look Around

Ask your students to stand without making a sound. Now tell them to:

- Close your eyes or look down at your hands as you feel yourself standing.

- Take three mindful breaths (leave some silence for them to enjoy).

- Feel your feet on the floor, feel the anchor of your breath.

- Now lift your eyes and slowly scan the room without speaking. How do you feel?

Sphere Breathing

Good to try with students before a test, a performance, or any stress-inducing event:

- Pretend you're holding a large balloon in both hands, with relaxed elbows.

- Now inhale and gently pull your fingers apart so there's plenty of space between your fingers.

- Now exhale and slowly bring your fingers back to gently touch.

- After a few cycles of breath, close your eyes and notice if you can bring your fingers back precisely.

- Repeat a few times. This can be fun and challenging!

Bean bag on tummy activity: While lying down with eyes closed, breathe and feel bean bag move.

Watch Calming Meditation Videos Online[3]

Smelling a flower (inhale, take in breath); blowing out a candle (exhale, release breath).

Count up to 5 as you breathe in; count backwards from 5 as you breathe out.

Pretend your belly is a balloon: breathe in to inflate it, breathe out to deflate it.

Video: "Sesame Street Belly Breathing Activity with Elmo"[4]

Video: "Reading of *Puppy Mind* by Andrew Nance"[5]

Video: "4-7-8 Breathing Exercise by GoZen"[6]

- An animated demonstration of a breathing strategy.

Poster, Mindfulness On-the-Go, breathing steps using the road metaphor.[2]

MINDFULNESS
ON THE GO

1. Bring your attention into your body.

2. Breathe in through your nose and let your abdomen expand fully.

3. Breathe out through your mouth.

4. Notice each inhale and exhale.

5. Proceed slowly with the task at hand. Take pleasure in sight, sound and touch.

6. Savor every sensation.

#mindfulschools

Breathing Sticks[7]

- String 5 beads, or your choice of number of beads, onto a pipe cleaner.

- Use finger to move each bead with a new breath.

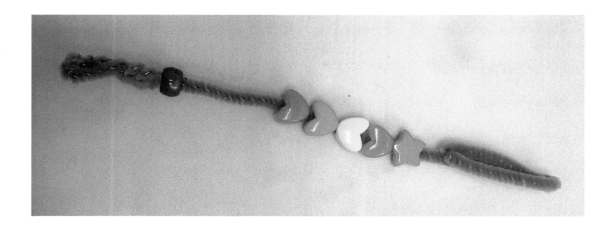

Power Breath (HA! breath)

- Arms up to the sky.

- Grab energy from the sun.

- Bring arms and fist to chest, saying "HA!"

- Grab the energy and pull it into your chest.

Breathing Buddies

Make these with students to take home or make them at home to self-calm.

Materials: fun socks (one for each student), pillow stuffing, rubber bands (5 for each Buddy), soft chenille bendable sticks or pipe cleaners (2 for each Buddy), sharpies.

- Each student gets 1 sock.

- Each student gets stuffing to put inside the sock; after the head of the Buddy is full, add a rubber band.

- Repeat above step 4 times so the Buddy has 5 bumps. Tie off the top of the sock.

- Using a sharpie, have the child draw a face on the toe-end of the sock.

- Add chenille sticks for antennae or bows.

- Practice breathing: using one finger, slide slowly over each bump. Breathe deeply for each bump on the Buddy.

Spaghetti Activity

Uncooked: stand still and rigid, hands at the side, fists clenched and tight.

Cooked: flop around, move limbs loosely.

How do you feel? Emphasize stressed and tense vs. relaxed and calm.

Books and Resources

Good Night Yoga

Peaceful Piggy Yoga

Sitting Still Like a Frog (includes CD)

Mindful Movements: Ten Exercises for Well-Being (includes CD)

Planting Seeds: Practicing Mindfulness with Children (includes CD)

Puppy Mind by Andrew Nance[5]

"Yoga 4 Classrooms" Cards[8]

No Ordinary Apple (Mindful Eating)

Have You Filled a Bucket Today?

Breathe Like a Bear

Please see the Reference on page 107 for the exact url for articles, videos, and more.

Breathing Exercises Appendix: Mindful Breathing (page 119)

GRADES 3 & 4

Resources for Breathing and Body Awareness

GOAL OF THIS SECTION: BUILD AWARENESS OF BREATH AS A TOOL FOR SELF-REGULATION.

Hoberman Sphere

Video: Breathing with a Sphere by Elizabeth Miller[1]

Poster, Mindfulness On-the-Go, breathing steps using the road metaphor.[2]

Anchor Hand

Ask students to hold up their nondominant hand spreading fingers. Tell them to:

- Use the index finger of the hand you write with.

- Now trace each outspread finger in time with a full cycle of breath.

- Feel your tracing finger move up as you inhale, keep looking as your finger moves down the other side, and you exhale.

- When you get to the end of your hand, your thumb or finger, just reverse and keep on breathing and looking.

Slow Down, Look Around

Ask your students to stand without making a sound. Now tell them to:

- Close your eyes or look down at your hands as you feel yourself standing.

- Take three mindful breaths (leave some silence for them to enjoy).

- Feel your feet on the floor, feel the anchor of your breath.

- Now lift your eyes and slowly scan the room without speaking. How do you feel?

Sphere Breathing

Good to try with students before a test, a performance, or any stress-inducing event:

- Pretend you're holding a large balloon in both hands, with relaxed elbows.

- Now inhale and gently pull your fingers apart so there's plenty of space between your fingers.

- Now exhale and slowly bring your fingers back to gently touch.

- After a few cycles of breath, close your eyes and notice if you can bring your fingers back precisely.

- Repeat a few times. This can be fun and challenging!

Review and discuss "anchor words" or phrases and how to use them; Example: "breathe in, breathe out"

Draw pictures of a Non-Mindful body and a Mindful body.

Poster, <u>Mindfulness On-the-Go</u>, breathing steps using the road metaphor.[2]

Breathing Sticks[7]

- String 5 beads, or your choice of number of beads, onto a pipe cleaner.

- Use finger to move each bead with a new breath.

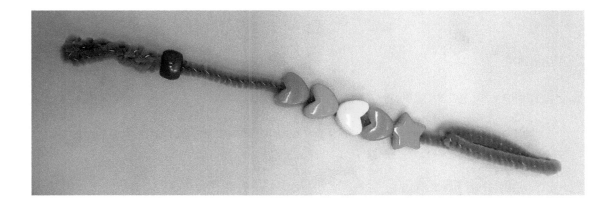

Thought Bubbles

- Students make or use their own picture of themselves with 4 "thought bubbles" or clouds around their head.

- Then, while practicing Mindful Breathing, write out the first 4 thoughts they have and write them in the thought bubbles.

- Continue this by filling in "thought bubbles" that say: "A thought I don't want to have," "A thought I have over and over," and "A new thought."

4-7-8 Breathing[6]

- Breathe in 4.

- Hold for 7.

- Breathe out 8.

Spaghetti Activity

Uncooked: stand still and rigid, hands at the side, fists clenched and tight.

Cooked: flop around, move limbs loosely.

How do you feel? Emphasize stressed and tense vs. relaxed and calm.

Slow Motion

- Write your name 10 times as slowly as you can.

- Notice all the sensations you feel in your shoulders, arms, hand, and fingers.

Power Breath (HA! breath)

- Arms up to the sky.

- Grab energy from the sun.

- Bring arms and fist to chest, saying "HA!"

- Grab the energy and pull it into your chest.

Do a body scan *(see Breathing Exercises Appendix: Mindful Breathing on page 119)*.

Use visuals of each part of the body when guiding the scan.

Kid Relaxation (Heart Breath activity)

- Make a heart with your hands.

- Hold to your own heart.

- Big Bear Hug - Hug Yourself!

Kids Relaxation - Parents/Educators' Blog for resources, ideas, and activities for relaxation[9]

Watch Calming Meditation Videos Online[3]

Watch Guided Meditations for Mindfulness Videos Online[10]

Breathing Buddies

Make these with students to take home or make them at home to self-calm.

Materials: fun socks (one for each student), pillow stuffing, rubber bands (5 for each Buddy), soft chenille bendable sticks or pipe cleaners (2 for each Buddy), sharpies.

- Each student gets 1 sock.

- Each student gets stuffing to put inside the sock; after the head of the Buddy is full, add a rubber band.

- Repeat above step 4 times so the Buddy has 5 bumps. Tie off the top of the sock.

- Using a sharpie, have the child draw a face on the toe-end of the sock.

- Add chenille sticks for antennae or bows.

- Practice breathing: using one finger, slide slowly over each bump. Breathe deeply for each bump on the Buddy.

Books and Resources

Good Night Yoga

Peaceful Piggy Yoga

Sitting Still Like a Frog (includes CD)

Mindful Movements: Ten Exercises for Well-Being (includes CD)

Planting Seeds: Practicing Mindfulness with Children (includes CD)

Breathe Like a Bear

"Yoga 4 Classrooms" Cards[8]

Please see the Reference on page 107 for the exact url for articles, videos, and more.

Breathing Exercises Appendix: Mindful Breathing (page 119)

GRADES 5 & 6

Resources for Breathing and Body Awareness

GOAL OF THIS SECTION: BUILD AWARENESS OF BREATH AS A TOOL FOR SELF-REGULATION.

Songs and Raps on Mindfulness

Video: <u>Don't Flip Yo' Lid</u> By Fabian Jackson and Glenview Elementary, Madison, WI[11]

<u>Taming the Palace Guard One Breath at a Time by The Mindful Classroom</u>[12]

<u>Video: Calm Down and Release Amygdala</u>[13]

Do a Body Scan or Mindful Breathing: Use visuals of each part of the body when guiding the scan.

Handwriting Activity

- Write your name with your nondominant hand.

- Discuss the challenges.

- What do you have to be aware of?

- How do your mind and focus change?

"Still Chillin'"

- Sitting in a circle, students are timed in intervals of 5 minutes to see who can be completely still the longest.

"Pass the Cup of Water"

- Students pass a filled cup of water to each other without spilling.

- Try doing it with eyes closed.

Video: "Just Breathe" by Julie Bayer Salzman & Josh Salzman[14]

Spaghetti Activity

Uncooked: stand still and rigid, hands at the side, fists clenched and tight.

Cooked: flop around, move limbs loosely.

How do you feel? Emphasize stressed and tense vs. relaxed and calm.

Breathing Sticks[7]

- String 5 beads, or your choice of number of beads, onto a pipe cleaner.

- Use finger to move each bead with a new breath.

4-7-8 Breathing[6]

- Breathe in 4.

- Hold for 7.

- Breathe out 8.

Glitter Jar *(see Glitter Jar sample on page 23 or 31)*

Breathing Exercises Appendix: Mindful Breathing (page 119)

Breathing Exercises Appendix: Mindful Breathing (page 120)

Books and Resources

Sitting Still Like a Frog (includes CD) for younger kids but good for stories and "starters"

Mindful Movements: Ten Exercises for Well-Being (includes CD)

Planting Seeds: Practicing Mindfulness with Children (includes CD)

"Yoga 4 Classrooms" Cards "Growing Mindful" cards[8]

"A Still Quiet Place for Teens" Workbook (Grade 6 only)[41]

"Mindfulness for Teen Anxiety" Workbook (Grade 6 only)[40]

Mindful Coloring Cover[15]

Mindful Coloring Pages[15b]

Please see the Reference on page 107 for the exact url for articles, videos, and more.

Breathing Exercises Appendix: Mindful Breathing (page 119)

Breathing Exercises Appendix: Mindful Breathing (page 120)

GRADES 7 & 8

Resources for Breathing and Body Awareness

GOAL OF THIS SECTION: BUILD AWARENESS OF BREATH AS A TOOL FOR SELF-REGULATION.

Hoberman Sphere

Video: Breathing with a Sphere by Elizabeth Miller[1]

Breathing Sticks[7]

- String 5 beads, or your choice of number of beads, onto a pipe cleaner.

- Use finger to move each bead with a new breath.

4-7-8 Breathing[6]

- Breathe in 4.

- Hold for 7.

- Breathe out 8.

Videos, Audios, Guided Meditations, Articles

"Release" Original Film on Middle School Anxiety by Mindful Schools[16] (5:45 mins)

"NBA's Winningest Team Guided by Mindfulness and Joy"[17]

Releasing Fear – (try this script, repeat) "Breathe in calm. Breathe out worry. Breathe in peace. Breathe out fear."

"The Mindful Athlete with George Mumford - 10 minute Guided Meditation"[18]

"How NBA Coach Phil Jackson Taught His Players to Use Mindfulness"[19] (5:00 mins)

Jade Meadow: "A Guided Visualization Teens LOVE"[20] (4:30 mins)

Mindfulness Teen: "SOBER Breathing Space (Stop, Observe, Breathe, Expand & Respond)"[21] (3:00 mins)

"8 Hour Deep Sleeping Music: Delta Waves, Relaxing Music Sleep, Insomnia Music, Meditation"[22]

Using a Glitter Jar

"Settling Our Glitter"

- Watch glitter settle and compare to thoughts experienced.

- Use as a timer - 1 1/2 to 2 minutes. Then start class.

- Shake jar, breathe mindfully until glitter settles.

"Still Chillin'"

- Sitting in a circle, students are timed in intervals of 5 minutes to see who can be completely still the longest.

"Pass the Cup of Water"

- Students pass a filled cup of water to each other without spilling.

- Try doing it with eyes closed.

Please see the Reference on page 107 for the exact url for articles, videos, and more.

Breathing Exercises Appendix: Mindful Breathing (page 119)

K - 2

Resources for Awareness of Emotions

GOAL OF THIS SECTION: RECOGNIZE THE RANGE OF FEELINGS, DIFFICULTIES, AND NEEDS IN OURSELVES AND OTHERS.

Activities

Worry Hanger Students think of a worry, draw a picture of it, and hang it on the Worry Hanger. Teacher puts the Worry Hanger aside, may refer to it later for discussion and sharing.

Glitter Jar *(see Glitter Jar sample on page 23 or 31)* Have students think of 4-6 emotions. Have them write them down if they can. Then have them draw what they think the emotions look like on a blank face.

Facial Expressions and Emotions Demonstrate facial expressions and what emotions they show. Mirror facial expressions. Example: Teacher shows surprised face, student makes same face. Students can do the same activity with a partner.

Video: Dr. Daniel Siegel presenting a Hand Model of the Brain[23]

- Dr. Daniel Siegel demonstrates how the hand can be used as a model for the brain to help better understand emotions.

How our emotions can change. Use metaphors.

Example: the weather, using the remote control, gears on a car, light switch, velcro/teflon.

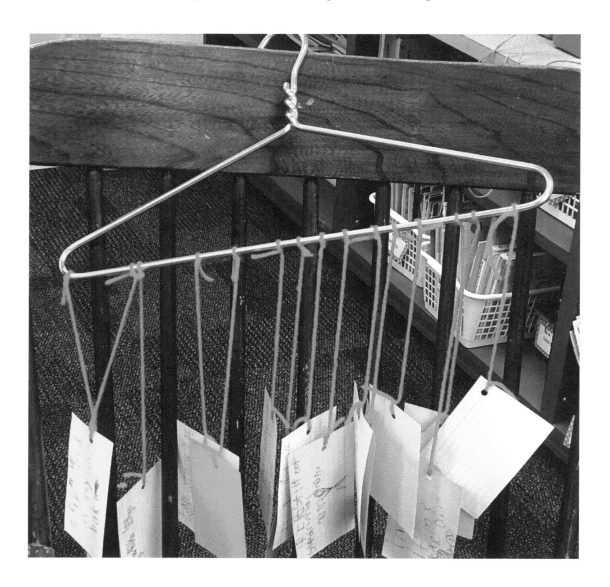

Make Your Personal Remote - "Change Your Channel" (this image teaches kids that they can "pause" and "choose" a different "channel" or emotion. The buttons help children begin to better identify their emotions and what they can do to manage them. See *Remote sample* on page 33).

Videos, Audios, Guided Meditations, Articles

Sesame Street: Bruno Mars: "Don't Give Up"[24]

Sesame Street: "Me Want It (But Me Wait)" - Impulse control with Cookie Monster[25]

Sesame Street: "Feelings"[26]

Sesame Street: "Bert Gets Angry"[27]

"The Feelings Song"[28]

Sesame Street: "Belly Breathing Activity with Elmo"[4]

   (also used for breathing but has an anger component)

Others

Feelings Song for Children by The Learning Station (Sad, Bad, Terrible Day)[29]

Controlling Emotions: A Lesson from Angry Birds[30]

How Mindfulness Empowers Us: An Animation Narrated by Sharon Salzberg[31]

The Struggle Switch - by Dr. Russ Harris[32]

Watch Calming Meditation Videos Online[3]

Mindful Coloring (Cover / Inside Pages)[15 + 15B]

Please see the Reference on page 107 for the exact url for articles, videos, and more.

Breathing Exercises Appendix: Mindful Breathing – Emotions (page 121)

GRADES 3 & 4

Resources for Awareness of Emotions

GOAL OF THIS SECTION: RECOGNIZE THE RANGE OF FEELINGS, DIFFICULTIES, AND NEEDS IN OURSELVES AND OTHERS.

Videos, Audios, Guided Meditations, Articles

How Mindfulness Empowers Us: An Animation Narrated by Sharon Salzberg[31]

Controlling Emotions: A Lesson from Angry Birds[30]

Calm Down and Release Amygdala Video[13]

Feelings Song for Children by The Learning Station (Sad, Bad, Terrible Day)[29]

Sesame Street: Bruno Mars: "Don't Give Up"[24]

Sesame Street: "Me Want It (But Me Wait)" - Impulse control with Cookie Monster[25]

Sesame Street: "Feelings"[26]

Sesame Street: "Bert Gets Angry"[27]

"The Feelings Song"[28]

The Struggle Switch - by Dr. Russ Harris[21]

Watch Calming Meditation Videos Online[3]

Activities

Worry Hanger

- Students think of a worry.

- Draw a picture or write it down.

- Hang it on the Worry Hanger.

Glitter Jar, Watching Your Thoughts.

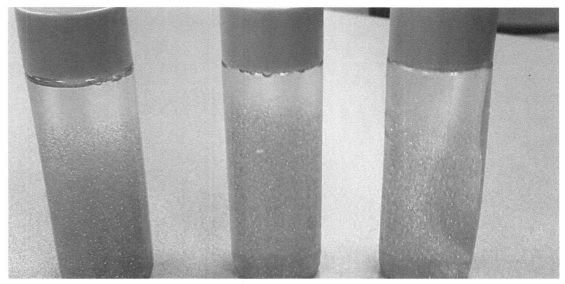

Have students think of 4-6 emotions. Have them write them if they can. Then have them draw what they think the emotions look like on a blank face.

Facial Expressions and Emotions

- Teacher shows surprised face, student makes same face.

- Students can do the same activity with a partner.

- Look at pictures of people's facial expressions, try and guess the emotion.

Emoji Samples

Look at some and try to guess the emotion. Students can make their own emoji.

Metaphors for Emotions

Examples: the weather, using the remote control, gears on a car, light switch, velcro/teflon.

Wheel of Awareness[33]

Bicycle wheel diagram demonstrates how our emotions shift from negative to positive *(see page 41)*

Video: Dr. Daniel Siegel presenting a Hand Model of the Brain[23] (demonstrates how the hand can be used as a model for the brain to help better understand emotions)

Video: Marshmallow Test - Increase student understanding of impulse control[34]

Kids Relaxation Activities Blog[8]

Mindful Coloring (Cover / Inside Pages)[15 + 15B]

Make Your Personal Remote - "Change Your Channel"

- This image teaches kids that they can "pause" and "choose" a different channel (or emotion).

- The buttons help children begin to better Identify their emotions and what they can do to manage them.

- This is a simple template meant to provide an example, students can also make their own.

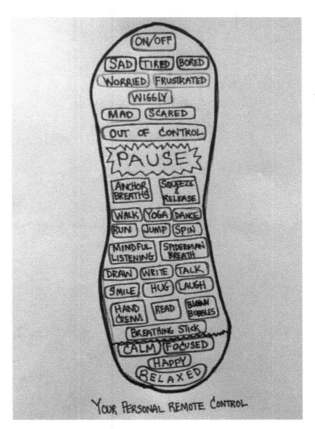

Videos

How Mindfulness Empowers Us: An Animation Narrated by Sharon Salzberg[31]

Controlling Emotions: A Lesson from Angry Birds[30]

Calm Down and Release Amygdala Video[13]

Feelings Song for Children by The Learning Station (Sad, Bad, Terrible Day)[29]

Sesame Street: Bruno Mars: "Don't Give Up"[24]

Sesame Street: "Me Want It (But Me Wait)" - Impulse control with Cookie Monster[25]

Sesame Street: "Feelings"[26]

Sesame Street: "Bert Gets Angry"[27]

"The Feelings Song"[28]

The Struggle Switch - by Dr. Russ Harris[21]

Watch Calming Meditation Videos Online[3]

Please see the Reference on page 107 for the exact url for articles, videos, and more.

Breathing Exercises Appendix: Mindful Breathing – Emotions (Page 121)

GRADES 5 & 6

Resources for Awareness of Emotions

GOAL OF THIS SECTION: RECOGNIZE THE RANGE OF FEELINGS, DIFFICULTIES, AND NEEDS IN OURSELVES AND OTHERS.

Activities

Guided Meditations by Mindfulness for Teens[35]

Video: Dr. Daniel Siegel presenting a Hand Model of the Brain[23] (demonstrates how the hand can be used as a model for the brain to help better understand emotions)

Wheel of Awareness[33]

Bicycle wheel diagram demonstrates how our emotions shift from negative to positive *(see page 41)*

Emoji Samples

Find emojis of different emotions online and create individual ones.

Limit colors to yellow, red, blue, and black (see page 32).

Glitter Jar, Watching Your Thoughts.

"Worry Wads"

- Write a worry on a piece of paper.

- Crumple it and throw it in the middle of the room.

- Write your worry and make it a paper airplane to fly away.

Science

Getting to Know and Love Your Brain Poster by Scholastic[36]

- Information on how DNA can be changed positively and negatively by emotions

Gaia - Missing Links: Connections[37] (1:23 min)

Calm Down and Release Amygdala[13] (6:40 min)

- Information on the amygdala the part of our brain that controls emotions, and how it can be calmed down.

Neuroplasticity by Sentis[38] (2:03 min)

Videos

Controlling Emotions: A Lesson from Angry Birds[30]

Marshmallow Test - Increase student understanding of impulse control[34]

Sesame Street: "Me Want It (But Me Wait)" - Impulse control with Cookie Monster[25]

The Struggle Switch - by Dr. Russ Harris - Metaphor of the use of switches to

decrease anxiety[32]

How Mindfulness Empowers Us: An Animation Narrated by Sharon Salzberg[31]

- Story of two wolves shows how mindfulness can empower us.

Please see the Reference on page 107 for the exact url for articles, videos, and more.

Breathing Exercises Appendix: Mindful Breathing – Emotions (page 121)

GRADES 7 & 8

Resources for Awareness of Emotions

GOAL OF THIS SECTION: RECOGNIZE THE RANGE OF FEELINGS, DIFFICULTIES, AND NEEDS IN OURSELVES AND OTHERS.

<u>Whip-Around</u>

- Everyone take a moment to notice how you are feeling right now.

- See if there is one word that describes the feeling.

- It may be calm, energetic, bored, interested, happy, irritated, or another feeling.

- Now we will do a "Whip-Around" to share that one word, so as I point to you, just say your one word.

- If you really don't want to share, is there a word that describes that?

- If you pay close attention, the way you feel right now might actually change by the time it is your turn.

79th Organ (Exchange Phone Activity)

- We have 78 organs, all of which we need to maintain health. To lose one causes pain. Our smartphones are our 79th organ.

- Have students look at their turned-off phone.

- Notice it. Notice emotions, urges, body response to it.

- Turn on the phone.

- Swap with a partner, then notice feelings.

- After a minute, tell students to switch back.

- Share and reflect what feelings occurred, what was felt? Why?

Boredom!

- Discuss what it feels like to be bored (not a good feeling).

- Share that being bored is really a choice.

- Tell the story about a scientist who was asked how he could not become bored looking at cells and DNA strands all day. He responded that he is always looking for something new when he looks at stuff through the microscope. He said that by turning up his own curiosity, he starts to find things interesting, and is not bored.

- Ask students to share things that they find interesting that might bore others.

- Then ask if there is a way to do what the scientist did to turn up curiosity and look and listen, to make things more interesting.

- End with saying the next time you are feeling bored, notice how it feels in your body and mind. Can you see things from a different perspective?

Wheel of Awareness[33]

Bicycle wheel diagram demonstrates how our emotions shift from negative to positive.

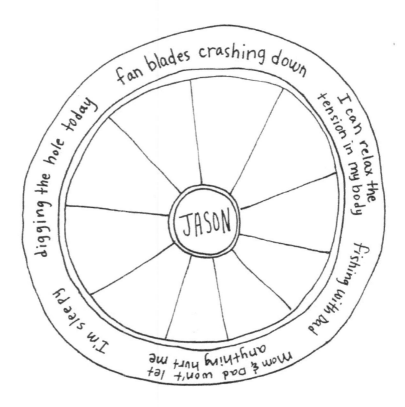

Breathing Exercises Appendix: Mindful Breathing – Emotions (page 121)

Videos

Amygdala Hijack & Emotional Intelligence[39]

Marshmallow Test - Increase student understanding of impulse control[34]

Books

Mindfulness for Teen Anxiety: A Workbook for Overcoming Anxiety at Home, at School and Everywhere Else by Christopher Willard[40]

A Still Quiet Place for Teens: A Mindfulness Workbook to Ease Stress and Difficult Emotions by Amy Saltzman[41]

Guided Meditations

Mindfulness of Emotions Meditation[42] (10 mins)

Watch Calming Meditation Videos Online[3]

Watch Guided Meditations for Mindfulness Videos Online[9]

Please see the Reference on page 107 for the exact url for articles, videos, and more.

Teen Stressors

- Circle a word, discuss, share, post, and add more.

K -2

Resources for Heartfulness and Gratitude

GOAL OF THIS SECTION: DEVELOP AN APPRECIATION OF THE GOOD IN OUR LIVES.

<u>Open Heart/Closed Heart</u>

- Tape a simple paper heart on the front of a small stuffed animal.

- Fold over the heart to show it is closed.

- Unfold the heart to show that it is open.

- Share ideas on what this means.

<u>Video: Sesame Street: Mark Ruffalo: Empathy</u>[43]

Use role play to show friendship and caring for someone's feelings.

Use "<u>Yoga 4 Classrooms</u>" Card Set for examples of Community and Heartful exercises and activities[8]

"Web of Kindness"

- Students sit in a circle.

- Teacher begins rolling a ball of yarn to a student while giving them a compliment.

- Modeling the teacher, students take turns rolling the yarn.

- This will create a "Web of Kindness."

- Heartful messages can be sent. Example: "May You Be Happy."

Have students write down kind acts they have received, or create a list on the board. Challenge the class to see if they can write 50 for the week.

Think of kind things to say to each classmate or use one positive characteristic to describe someone.

Use the Classroom Heartfulness Jar when something kind is done. Add a stone for each act of kindness.

Kid Relaxation (Heart Breath activity)

- Make a heart with your hands.

- Hold to your own heart.

- Big Bear Hug - Hug Yourself!

Mindful Coloring (Cover / Inside Pages)[15 + 15B]

Video: How Mindfulness Empowers Us: An Animation Narrated by Sharon Salzberg[31]

- Story of two wolves shows how mindfulness can empower us.

Have You Filled a Bucket Today? by Carol McCloud[44]

"How to Fill Your Bucket" by Lisa Marie Performing Arts - Follow Up Lesson[45]

Please see the Reference on page 107 for the exact url for articles, videos, and more.

Morning Meeting Activity

Have students complete the following phrase:

- "I am grateful for . . ." or "Find the Good."

- Remind students that during the day when they are upset, they can think back to something they are grateful for.

Who Helped You Today?

Ask the students the following questions:

- How did each activity of your day occur?

- How did someone make that happen?

- Show gratitude for each person that impacted your day.

Gratitude Scavenger Hunt

- List people and things you are grateful for.

Examples:

- Someone in my family.

- A friend.

- Something in my room.

- My classroom.

- My neighborhood.

- Favorite thing like a blanket, a book, a game, a special food.

Gratitude Rocks

Paint and decorate a rock for the classroom that represents gratitude.

- Collect small rocks such as landscaping rocks.

- Students personalize the rocks by painting, writing, and decorating.

- Students keep the rocks in their desk, pocket, or special place to remind them to be grateful.

Classroom Gratitude Rock

- Using a large rock, follow the steps listed previously to create a collaborative rock for the classroom. Place it on the teacher's desk or other central place in the room.

Classroom Gratitude Jar

- When students are grateful for something, they put a stone in the jar.

Please see the Reference on page 107 for the exact url for articles, videos, and more.

GRADES 3 & 4

Resources for Heartfulness and Gratitude

GOAL OF THIS SECTION: DEVELOP AN APPRECIATION OF THE GOOD IN OUR LIVES.

Open Heart/Closed Heart

- Tape a simple paper heart on the front of a small stuffed animal.

- Fold over the heart to show it is closed.

- Unfold the heart to show that it is open.

- Share ideas on what this means.

Video: Sesame Street: Mark Ruffalo: Empathy[43]

Use role play to show friendship and caring for someone's feelings.

Use "Yoga 4 Classrooms" Card Set for examples of Community and Heartful exercises and activities[8]

"Web of Kindness"

- Students sit in a circle.

- Teacher begins rolling a ball of yarn to a student while giving them a compliment.

- Modeling the teacher, students take turns rolling the yarn.

- This will create a "Web of Kindness."

- Heartful messages can be sent. Example: "May You Be Happy."

Have students write down kind acts they have received, or create a list on the board. Challenge the class to see if they can write 50 for the week.

Think of kind things to say to each classmate or use one positive characteristic to describe someone.

Add a stone to the Classroom Heartfulness Jar when something kind is done.

Kid Relaxation (Heart Breath activity)

- Make a heart with your hands.

- Hold to your own heart.

- Big Bear Hug - Hug Yourself!

Mindful Coloring (Cover / Inside Pages)[15 + 15B]

Video: How Mindfulness Empowers Us: An Animation Narrated by Sharon Salzberg[31]

- Story of two wolves shows how mindfulness can empower us.

Have You Filled a Bucket Today? by Carol McCloud[44]

Please see the Reference on page 107 for the exact url for articles, videos, and more.

Who Helped You Today?

Ask the students the following questions:

- How did each activity of your day occur?

- How did someone make that happen?

- Show gratitude for each person that impacted your day.

Gratitude Scavenger Hunt

- List people and things you are grateful for.

Examples:

- Someone in my family.

- A friend.

- Something in my room.

- My classroom.

- My neighborhood.

- Favorite thing like a blanket, a book, a game, a special food.

Gratitude Rocks

Paint and decorate a rock for the classroom that represents gratitude.

- Collect small rocks such as landscaping rocks.

- Students personalize the rocks by painting, writing, and decorating.

- Students keep the rocks in their desk, pocket, or special place to remind them to be grateful.

Classroom Gratitude Rock

- Using a large rock, follow the steps listed previously to create a collaborative rock for the classroom. Place it on the teacher's desk or other central place in the room.

Classroom Gratitude Jar

- When students are grateful for something, they put a stone in the jar.

Please see the Reference on page 107 for the exact url for articles, videos, and more.

Breathing Exercises Appendix: Mindful Breathing – Heartfulness (page 122)

Breathing Exercises Appendix: Mindful Breathing – Gratitude (page 123)

GRADES 5 & 6

Resources for Heartfulness and Gratitude

GOAL OF THIS SECTION: DEVELOP AN APPRECIATION OF THE GOOD IN OUR LIVES.

Have You Filled a Bucket Today? by Carol McCloud[44]

"How to Fill Your Bucket" by Lisa Marie Performing Arts - Follow Up Lesson[45]

Heartfulness Cards

Use index cards, designed to send out a kind thought.

- "May you be . . ." and add "happy," "peaceful," or "safe."

- Use heart stickers, colored pencils, or markers to decorate the cards.

Classroom Gratitude Jar

- When students are grateful for something, they put a stone in the jar.

Kid Relaxation (Heart Breath activity)

- Make a heart with your hands.

- Hold to your own heart.

- While breathing, send out heartful thoughts.

Beach Ball Toss

- Teacher tosses a ball to a student and gives them a compliment.

- Students continue to toss ball to each other and compliment their classmates.

- Another option is to send a kind message. Example: "May you be happy."

- Alternative activity is to play the Beach Ball Toss using a piece of paper to pass around for each student.

Video: How Mindfulness Empowers Us: An Animation Narrated by Sharon Salzberg[31]
Story of two wolves shows how mindfulness can empower us.

Gratitude Journal

Keep a classroom Gratitude Journal for students.

The Gratitude Experiment Video[46] (4:43 min)
Some science and good ideas for Journal writing lists.

Gratitude Rocks

Paint and decorate a rock for the classroom that represents gratitude.

- Collect small rocks such as landscaping rocks.

- Students personalize the rocks by painting, writing, and decorating.

- Students keep the rocks in their desk, pocket, or special place to remind them to be grateful.

Classroom Gratitude Rock

- Using a large rock, follow the steps listed previously to create a collaborative rock for the classroom. Place it on the teacher's desk or other central place in the room.

Classroom Gratitude Jar

- When students are grateful for something, they put a stone in the jar.

Gratitude Activity: 'Hunt the Good' to Find Happiness[47]

- "Every Day May Not Be Good, but There Is Something Good in Every Day."

"How to Reduce Stress with Gratitude" Inspirational Reading by Nataly Kogan[48]

Mindfulness Exercise for Teachers - Gratitude Visualization

Today, commit to looking at your everyday scenery through the eyes of a child. For a moment, connect with the overlooked sensations of your environment - the warm feeling of your coffee cup, the smell of the rain, the colors of the fall trees. Notice the way your body responds to the various stimuli with a sense of gratitude.

Meditations

Friendly Wishes by Annaka Harris - Guided Meditations[49] (4:20 mins)

GoZen! Loving-Kindness Meditation[50] (4:54 mins)

Gratitude Meditation (Strengthen Happiness) by Stop, Breathe & Think[51] (5:30 mins)

Please see the Reference on page 107 for the exact url for articles, videos, and more.

Breathing Exercises Appendix: Mindful Breathing – Heartfulness (page 122)

Breathing Exercises Appendix: Mindful Breathing – Gratitude (page 123)

GRADES 7 & 8

Resources for Heartfulness and Gratitude

GOAL OF THIS SECTION: DEVELOP AN APPRECIATION OF THE GOOD IN OUR LIVES.

Beach Ball Toss

- Teacher tosses a ball to a student and gives them a compliment.

- Students continue to toss ball to each other and compliment their classmates.

- Another option is to send a kind message. Example: "May you be happy."

- Alternative activity is to play the Beach Ball Toss using a piece of paper to pass around for each student.

Gratitude Activity: 'Hunt the Good' to Find Happiness[47]

- "Every Day May Not Be Good, but There Is Something Good in Every Day."

"How to Reduce Stress with Gratitude" Inspirational Reading by Nataly Kogan[48]

The Self-Compassion Workbook for Teens - *Mindfulness & Compassion*

Skills to Overcome Self-Criticism & Embrace Who You Are by Karen Bluth[52]

Mindfulness Exercise - Gratitude Visualization

Today, commit to looking at your everyday scenery through the eyes of a child. For a moment, connect with the overlooked sensations of your environment - the warm feeling of your coffee cup, the smell of the rain, the colors of the fall trees. Notice the way your body responds to the various stimuli with a sense of gratitude.

Meditations

Friendly Wishes by Annaka Harris - Guided Meditations[49] (4:20 mins)

GoZen! Loving-Kindness Meditation[50] (4:54 mins)

Gratitude Meditation (Strengthen Happiness) by Stop, Breathe & Think[51] (5:30 mins)

Please see the Reference on page 107 for the exact url for articles, videos, and more.

Breathing Exercises Appendix: Mindful Breathing – Heartfulness (page 122)

Breathing Exercises Appendix: Mindful Breathing – Gratitude (page 123)

GRADES K - 2

Resources for Listening and Positive Communication

GOAL OF THIS SECTION: DEVELOP AWARENESS OF SOUND AND CULTIVATE POSITIVE WAYS TO COMMUNICATE.

The Singing Bowl

For a minute, listen to sounds in 3 places: classroom, outside your body, inside your body.

- Have students sit in a circle.

- Teacher rings the singing bowl.

- As students hear the chime, they count off in their head until they hear the sound.

- Pass the bowl around as it chimes and see if it can get back to the first person before the sound stops.

Bumble Bee Breath - "Yoga 4 Classrooms" Activity[8]

- Close your eyes.

- Breathe slowly and deeply through your nose.

- Exhale out to "hummmmm" as long as you can.

- Hear the sound and feel vibration.

Variation on this practice - cover your ears and use other sounds: "zzzzzzz," "shhhhhh," and "sssssss."

- Now what sounds do you hear?

Guide students through a Council Practice. Practice mindfulness through deep listening in a safe place that begins with a story, a quote or a question, speaker holds an object, discussion follows.

Reflection Opportunities

Teacher says "Mindful listening means you stop, reflect, and speak from the heart."

Ask students "What does this mean?"

Teacher says "Mindfulness means, it is the *intention* to *pay attention.*"

Ask students "What does this mean?"

From "*Pooh's Little Instruction Book*" by A.A. Milne[53], teacher quotes "Don't underestimate the value of doing nothing, of just going along, listening to all the things you can't hear, and not bothering."

Ask students "What does this mean?"

Music and Sound

- Play 3 different types of music (no lyrics) for 50-60 seconds each.

Examples: African drumming, upbeat instrumental, easy listening.

- Ask students "How does each type of music make your body feel?"

- Ask students "What awareness of your body did you have?"

Listening Eggs

- Fill colored eggs with different items small in size.

Examples: paper clips, pennies, buttons, various candies.

- Tell students to listen carefully.

- Shake each egg and have students guess what is inside.

- Can provide the choices on cards or on the smartboard to help with the guessing.

Please see the Reference on page 107 for the exact url for articles, videos, and more.

Breathing Exercises Appendix: Mindful Breathing – Listening (page 124)

GRADES 3 & 4

Resources for Listening and Positive Communication

GOAL OF THIS SECTION: DEVELOP AWARENESS OF SOUND AND CULTIVATE POSITIVE WAYS TO COMMUNICATE.

The Singing Bowl

For a minute, listen to sounds in 3 places: classroom, outside your body, inside your body.

- Have students sit in a circle.

- Teacher rings the singing bowl.

- As students hear the chime, they count off in their head until they hear the sound.

- Pass the bowl around as it chimes and see if it can get back to the first person before the sound stops.

Bumble Bee Breath - "Yoga 4 Classrooms" Activity[8]

- Close your eyes.

- Breathe slowly and deeply through your nose.

- Exhale out to "hummmmm" as long as you can.

- Hear the sound and feel vibration. Variation on this practice - cover your ears and use other sounds: "zzzzzzz," "shhhhhh," and "sssssss."

- Now what sounds do you hear?

Guide students through a Council Practice. Practice mindfulness through deep listening in a safe place that begins with a story, a quote or a question, speaker holds an object, discussion follows.

Read *Sick* by Shel Silverstein[54] and have students list as many of the 37 reasons as they can after one reading.

Reflection Opportunities

Teacher says "Mindful listening means you stop, reflect, and speak from the heart."

Ask students "What does this mean?"

Teacher says "Mindfulness means, it is the *intention* to *pay attention."*

Ask students "What does this mean?"

From "*Pooh's Little Instruction Book*" by A.A. Milne[53], teacher quotes "Don't underestimate the value of doing nothing, of just going along, listening to all the things you can't hear, and not bothering."

Ask students "What does this mean?"

Music and Sound

- Play 3 different types of music (no lyrics) for 50-60 seconds each.

Examples: African drumming, upbeat instrumental, easy listening.

- Ask students "How does each type of music make your body feel?"

- Ask students "What awareness of your body did you have?"

Listening Eggs

- Fill colored eggs with different items small in size.

Examples: paper clips, pennies, buttons, various candies.

- Tell students to listen carefully.

- Shake each egg and have students guess what is inside.

- Can provide the choices on cards or on the smartboard to help with the guessing.

Things to Post

Video: Forest Hill South Park Gratitude Video[55] (1:34)

After viewing, have students list the things the dad in the family is grateful for - from memory!

Learning The Four Gates of Speech - The Indian Sufi Tradition[56]

S.L.A.N.T. - Model, demonstrate, role play.[57]

- When you listen . . .

    - **S:** Sit up Straight

    - **L:** Lean Forward

    - **A:** Act Interested

    - **N:** Nod Occasionally

    - **T:** Track the Speaker

T.H.I.N.K. - Steps to take before you speak.[58]

- Before you Speak...

    - **T:** Is it True?

    - **H:** Is it Helpful?

    - **I:** Is it Inspiring?

    - **N:** Is it Necessary?

    - **K:** Is it Kind?

Music and Reflection

Relating music to emotions. Choose from the songs below and have students listen. Share what emotions they may feel when listening and watching.

Scary

Jaws Theme Song[59]

Sad

Sad Violin[60]

Angry

The Angry Birds Movie - Main Orchestra Theme Music Video[61]

Happy

Matoma - Wonderful Life (Mi Oh My)[62]

Cheerful and Upbeat Music - Happy Background Music[63]

Other activities related to music:

Katy Perry, "Firework" - A Capella Cover - Mike Tompkins - Beatbox[64]

Have students pick one of the instruments and listen to it throughout.

Please see the Reference on page 107 for the exact url for articles, videos, and more.

Breathing Exercises Appendix: Mindful Breathing – Listening (page 124)

GRADES 5 - 6

Resources for Listening and Positive Communication

GOAL OF THIS SECTION: DEVELOP AWARENESS OF SOUND AND CULTIVATE POSITIVE WAYS TO COMMUNICATE.

The Singing Bowl

For a minute, listen to sounds in 3 places: classroom, outside your body, inside your body.

- Have students sit in a circle.

- Teacher rings the singing bowl.

- As students hear the chime, they count off in their head until they no longer hear the sound;

- Pass the bowl around as it chimes and see if it can get back to the first person before the sound stops.

Bumble Bee Breath - "Yoga 4 Classrooms" Activity[8]

- Close your eyes.

- Breathe slowly and deeply through your nose.

- Exhale out to "hummmmm" as long as you can.

- Hear the sound and feel vibration. Variation on this practice - cover your ears and use other sounds: "zzzzzzz," "shhhhhh," and "ssssss."

- Now what sounds do you hear?

Guide students through a Council Practice. Practice mindfulness through deep listening in a safe place that begins with a story, a quote or a question, speaker holds an object, discussion follows.

Read *Sick* by Shel Silverstein[54] and have students list as many of the 37 reasons as they can after one reading.

Reflection Opportunities

Teacher says "Mindful listening means you stop, reflect, and speak from the heart."

Ask students "What does this mean?"

Teacher says "Mindfulness means, it is the *intention* to *pay attention.*"

Ask students "What does this mean?"

From "*Pooh's Little Instruction Book*" by A.A. Milne[53], teacher quotes "Don't underestimate the value of doing nothing, of just going along, listening to all the things you can't hear, and not bothering."

Ask students "What does this mean?"

Music and Sound

- Play 3 different types of music (no lyrics) for 50-60 seconds each.

Examples: African drumming, upbeat instrumental, easy listening.

- Ask students "How does each type of music make your body feel?"

- Ask students "What awareness of your body did you have?"

Listening Eggs

- Fill colored eggs with different items small in size.

Examples: paper clips, pennies, buttons, various candies.

- Tell students to listen carefully.

- Shake each egg and have students guess what is inside.

- Can provide the choices on cards or on the smartboard to help with the guessing.

Things to Post

Video: Forest Hill South Park Gratitude Video[55] (1:34)

- After viewing, have students list the things the dad in the family is grateful for - *from memory!*

Learning <u>The Four Gates of Speech - The Indian Sufi Tradition</u>[56]

<u>S.L.A.N.T.</u> - Model, demonstrate, role play.[57]

- When you listen . . .

    - **S:** Sit up Straight

    - **L:** Lean Forward

    - **A:** Act Interested

    - **N:** Nod Occasionally

    - **T:** Track the Speaker

<u>T.H.I.N.K.</u> - Steps to take before you speak.[58]

- Before you Speak...

    - **T:** Is it True?

    - **H:** Is it Helpful?

    - **I:** Is it Inspiring?

    - **N:** Is it Necessary?

    - **K:** Is it Kind?

Music and Reflection

Relating music to emotions. Choose from the songs below and have students listen. Share what emotions they may feel when listening and watching.

<u>Scary</u>

<u>Jaws Theme Song</u>[59]

Sad

Sad Violin[60]

Angry

The Angry Birds Movie - Main Orchestra Theme Music Video[61]

Happy

Matoma - Wonderful Life (Mi Oh My)[62]

Cheerful and Upbeat Music - Happy Background Music[63]

Other activities related to music:

Katy Perry, "Firework" - A Capella Cover - Mike Tompkins - Beatbox[64]

Have students pick one of the instruments and listen to it throughout.

Please see the Reference on page 107 for the exact url for articles, videos, and more.

GRADES 7 - 8

Resources for Listening and Positive Communication

GOAL OF THIS SECTION: DEVELOP AWARENESS OF SOUND AND CULTIVATE POSITIVE WAYS TO COMMUNICATE.

The Singing Bowl

For a minute, listen to sounds in 3 places: classroom, outside your body, inside your body.

- Have students sit in a circle.

- Teacher rings the singing bowl.

- As students hear the chime, they count off in their head until they no longer hear the sound;

- Pass the bowl around as it chimes and see if it can get back to the first person before the sound stops.

Bumble Bee Breath - "Yoga 4 Classrooms" Activity[8]

- Close your eyes.

- Breathe slowly and deeply through your nose.

- Exhale out to "hummmmm" as long as you can.

- Hear the sound and feel vibration. Variation on this practice - cover your ears and use other sounds: "zzzzzzz," "shhhhhh," and "sssssss."

- Now what sounds do you hear?

Guide students through a Council Practice. Practice mindfulness through deep listening in a safe place that begins with a story, a quote or a question, speaker holds an object, discussion follows.

Read *Sick* by Shel Silverstein[54] and have students list as many of the 37 reasons as they can after one reading.

Reflection Opportunities

Teacher says "Mindful listening means you stop, reflect, and speak from the heart."

Ask students "What does this mean?"

Teacher says "Mindfulness means, it is the *intention* to *pay attention.*"

Ask students "What does this mean?"

From "*Pooh's Little Instruction Book*" by A.A. Milne[53], teacher quotes "Don't underestimate the value of doing nothing, of just going along, listening to all the things you can't hear, and not bothering."

Ask students "What does this mean?"

Music and Sound

- Play 3 different types of music (no lyrics) for 50-60 seconds each.

Examples: African drumming, upbeat instrumental, easy listening.

- Ask students "How does each type of music make your body feel?"

- Ask students "What awareness of your body did you have?"

Listening Eggs

- Fill colored eggs with different items small in size.

Examples: paper clips, pennies, buttons, various candies.

- Tell students to listen carefully.

- Shake each egg and have students guess what is inside.

- Can provide the choices on cards or on the smartboard to help with the guessing.

Things to Post

Video: Forest Hill South Park Gratitude Video[55] (1:34)

- After viewing, have students list the things the dad in the family is grateful for - *from memory!*

Learning The Four Gates of Speech - The Indian Sufi Tradition[56]

S.L.A.N.T. - Model, demonstrate, role play.[57]

- When you listen . . .

    - **S:** Sit up Straight

    - **L:** Lean Forward

    - **A:** Act Interested

    - **N:** Nod Occasionally

    - **T:** Track the Speaker

T.H.I.N.K. - Steps to take before you speak.[58]

- Before you Speak...

    - **T:** Is it True?

    - **H:** Is it Helpful?

    - **I:** Is it Inspiring?

    - **N:** Is it Necessary?

    - **K:** Is it Kind?

Music and Reflection

Relating music to emotions. Choose from the songs below and have students listen. Share what emotions they may feel when listening and watching.

Scary

Jaws Theme Song[59]

Sad

Sad Violin[60]

Angry

The Angry Birds Movie - Main Orchestra Theme Music Video[61]

Happy

Matoma - Wonderful Life (Mi Oh My)[62]

Cheerful and Upbeat Music - Happy Background Music[63]

Other activities related to music:

Katy Perry, "Firework" - A Capella Cover - Mike Tompkins - Beatbox[64]

Have students pick one of the instruments and listen to it throughout.

Please see the Reference on page 107 for the exact url for articles, videos, and more.

Breathing Exercises Appendix: Mindful Breathing – Listening (page 124)

K - 4

Resources for Engagement of the Senses

GOAL OF THIS SECTION: NOTICE AND ENGAGE THE SENSES TO SETTLE BODY AND MIND.

Sense of Taste Game

Blindfolded Fruit Tasting Game by Mindful Littles[65]

Taste & Smell Videos

Sense of Taste & Smell - Our Tongue & Nose by MakeMeGenius[66]

How the Tongue Works by KidsHealth.org[67]

See Mindful Eating on page 84.

Using a Glitter Jar - "Settling Our Glitter"

- Watch and observe glitter settle.

- Assign various emotions, feelings or experiences to varied-colored glitter jars.

- Challenge students to keep their eyes on the jar only, using it as an anchor.

- After shaking the jar, time how long it takes for glitter to all settle.

- Using counting as an anchor that keeps focus on the breath.

- Remind students that 80% of what we learn comes through our eyes."

Mute the Video

- Turn down the volume on a video.

- Students view the video and create their own subtitles to share with the class.

- Helps students realize how important sound is to the emotional experience of what you are watching.

Sounds in History Research how the Telegraph or the S.O.S. Code used sound to enhance the appreciation of sound.

The Ice Cube Episode[68]

- Students hold an ice cube in their hands.

- Students close their eyes and experience the sensation of cold.

- Direct them to try not to react to the sensations reflexively.

- Notice the sensations and feelings as they arise.

- If the feelings get too intense, tell students to "breathe" through it.

- Challenge students to see how long they can hold it without dropping it.

Skin & Touch Videos

The Ice Cube Episode by Mindful Littles[68]

How Your Skin Works by KidsHealth.org[69]

Give Yourself a Three-Breath Hug. Students take a minute to hug their shoulders tightly, eyes closed.

Tactile Awareness

- Gather together materials that represent different textures.

- Examples: A paper napkin, a door knob, sandpaper, your favorite blanket.

- Discuss the differences in texture.

- Repeat the activity with eyes closed and guess the item they are touching.

Discuss how blind people read Braille.

Olfactory Awareness

- Students close their eyes.

- Light a fragrant candle.

- Have students share what they smell.

- Other examples: fruit, cinnamon, almond extract, vanilla, citrus, lilac, coffee.

Aroma Memories

- Using visualization, ask students to recall a memory when prompted by a certain aroma.

- Examples: Baking bread, cookies, frying bacon, burning wood, turkey at Thanksgiving, exhaust fumes, a favorite flower, soup on the stove.

Smell and Taste

- Discuss how smell and taste are related.

- When you have a cold and can't smell or taste your food, how does it make you feel?

- How does it affect your appetite?

Mindful Eating

Gum Chewing Activity

- Gather a variety of flavors of sugar-free gum.

- Give each student a piece to hold in their hand, and have them try to guess the flavor.

- With their eyes closed, students rest the gum on their tongue.

- DO NOT CHEW IT!

- After a few seconds students may begin to slowly chew the gum.

- As they chew, ask them to see if they can identify the flavor of the gum.

- With younger students you may tell them what the possible flavors may be.

- This can also be done with chocolate, raisins, mints or other small treats.

Read *"No Ordinary Apple"* by Sara Marlowe[70]

Please see the Reference on page 107 for the exact url for articles, videos, and more.

GRADES 5 - 6

Resources for Engagement
of the Senses

GOAL OF THIS SECTION: NOTICE AND ENGAGE THE
SENSES TO SETTLE BODY AND MIND.

Sense of Taste Game

Blindfolded Fruit Tasting Game by Mindful Littles[65]

Taste & Smell Videos

Sense of Taste & Smell - Our Tongue & Nose by MakeMeGenius[66]

How the Tongue Works by KidsHealth.org[67]

See Mindful Eating on page 90.

Using a Glitter Jar - "Settling Our Glitter"

- Watch and observe glitter settle.

- Assign various emotions, feelings or experiences to varied-colored glitter jars.

- Challenge students to keep their eyes on the jar only, using it as an anchor.

- After shaking the jar, time how long it takes for glitter to all settle.

- Using counting as an anchor that keeps focus on the breath.

- Remind students that 80% of what we learn comes through our eyes."

Mute the Video

- Turn down the volume on a video.

- Students view the video and create their own subtitles to share with the class.

- Helps students realize how important sound is to the emotional experience of what you are watching.

H.E.A.R.

A WAY TO CULTIVATE
DEEP LISTENING

(STOP) HALT

Halt whatever you are doing
and offer your full attention.

♡ ENJOY

Enjoy a breath as you choose
to receive whatever is being
communicated to you—want-
ed or unwanted.

(?) ASK

Ask yourself if you really
know what they mean and
if you don't, ask for clarifi-
cation. Instead of making
assumptions, bring openness
and curiosity to the interac-
tion. You might be surprised
at what you discover.

💬 REFLECT

Reflect back to them what you
heard. This tells them that you
were really listening.

Sounds in History Research how the Telegraph or the S.O.S. Code used sound to enhance the appreciation of sound.

The Ice Cube Episode[68]

- Students hold an ice cube in their hands.

- Students close their eyes and experience the sensation of cold.

- Direct them to try not to react to the sensations reflexively.

- Notice the sensations and feelings as they arise.

- If the feelings get too intense, tell students to "breathe" through it.

- Challenge students to see how long they can hold it without dropping it.

Skin & Touch Videos

The Ice Cube Episode by Mindful Littles[68]

How Your Skin Works by KidsHealth.org[69]

Give Yourself a Three-Breath Hug. Students take a minute to hug their shoulders tightly, eyes closed.

Tactile Awareness

- Gather together materials that represent different textures.

- Examples: A paper napkin, a door knob, sandpaper, your favorite blanket.

- Discuss the differences in texture.

- Repeat the activity with eyes closed and guess the item they are touching.

Discuss how blind people read Braille.

Olfactory Awareness

- Students close their eyes.

- Light a fragrant candle.

- Have students share what they smell.

- Other examples: fruit, cinnamon, almond extract, vanilla, citrus, lilac, coffee.

Aroma Memories

- Using visualization, ask students to recall a memory when prompted by a certain aroma.

- Examples: Baking bread, cookies, frying bacon, burning wood, turkey at Thanksgiving, exhaust fumes, a favorite flower, soup on the stove.

Smell and Taste

- Discuss how smell and taste are related.

- When you have a cold and can't smell or taste your food, how does it make you feel?

- How does it affect your appetite?

Mindful Eating

Gum Chewing Activity

- Gather a variety of flavors of sugar-free gum.

- Give each student a piece to hold in their hand, and have them try to guess the flavor.

- With their eyes closed, students rest the gum on their tongue.

- DO NOT CHEW IT!

- After a few seconds students may begin to slowly chew the gum.

- As they chew, ask them to see if they can identify the flavor of the gum.

- With younger students you may tell them what the possible flavors may be.

- This can also be done with chocolate, raisins, mints or other small treats.

Read _"No Ordinary Apple"_ by Sara Marlowe[70]

Sense of Smell

Please see the Reference on page 107 for the exact url for articles, videos, and more.

GRADES 7 - 8

Resources for Engagement of the Senses

GOAL OF THIS SECTION: NOTICE AND ENGAGE THE SENSES TO SETTLE BODY AND MIND.

Things to Post and Use for Discussion

S.L.A.N.T. - Model, demonstrate, role play.[57]

- When you listen . . .

    - **S:** Sit up Straight

    - **L:** Lean Forward

    - **A:** Act Interested

    - **N:** Nod Occasionally

    - **T:** Track the Speaker

T.H.I.N.K. - Steps to take before you speak.[58]

- Before you Speak...

- **T:** Is it True?

- **H:** Is it Helpful?

- **I:** Is it Inspiring?

- **N:** Is it Necessary?

- **K:** Is it Kind?

H.E.A.R. - A Way to Cultivate Deep Listening

Music and Reflection

Relating music to emotions. Choose from the songs below and have students listen. Share what emotions they may feel when listening and watching.

Scary

Jaws Theme Song[59]

Sad

Sad Violin[60]

Angry

The Angry Birds Movie - Main Orchestra Theme Music Video[61]

Happy

Matoma - Wonderful Life (Mi Oh My)[62]

Cheerful and Upbeat Music - Happy Background Music[63]

Other activities related to music:

Katy Perry, "Firework" - A Capella Cover - Mike Tompkins - Beatbox[64]

Have students pick one of the instruments and listen to it throughout.

Mute the Video

- Turn down the volume on a video.

- Students view the video and create their own subtitles to share with the class.

- Helps students realize how important sound is to the emotional experience of what you are watching.

Sounds in History Research how the Telegraph or the S.O.S. Code used sound to enhance the appreciation of sound.

Please see the Reference on page 107 for the exact url for articles, videos, and more.

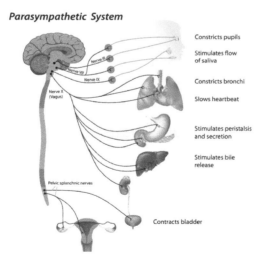

Parasympathetic System

Using a Glitter Jar - "Settling Our Glitter"

- Watch and observe glitter settle.

- Assign various emotions, feelings or experiences to varied-colored glitter jars.

- Challenge students to keep their eyes on the jar only, using it as an anchor.

- After shaking the jar, time how long it takes for glitter to all settle.

- Using counting as an anchor that keeps focus on the breath.

- Remind students that 80% of what we learn comes through our eyes."

Olfactory Awareness

- Students close their eyes.

- Light a fragrant candle.

- Have students share what they smell.

- Other examples: fruit, cinnamon, almond extract, vanilla, citrus, lilac, coffee.

Aroma Memories

- Using visualization, ask students to recall a memory when prompted by a certain aroma.

- Examples: Baking bread, cookies, frying bacon, burning wood, turkey at Thanksgiving, exhaust fumes, a favorite flower, soup on the stove.

Smell and Taste

- Discuss how smell and taste are related.

- When you have a cold and can't smell or taste your food, how does it make you feel?

- How does it affect your appetite?

The Ice Cube Episode[68]

- Students hold an ice cube in their hands.

- Students close their eyes and experience the sensation of cold.

- Direct them to try not to react to the sensations reflexively.

- Notice the sensations and feelings as they arise.

- If the feelings get too intense, tell students to "breathe" through it.

- Challenge students to see how long they can hold it without dropping it.

Give Yourself a Three-Breath Hug. Students take a minute to hug their shoulders tightly, eyes closed.

Tactile Awareness

- Gather together materials that represent different textures.

- Examples: A paper napkin, a door knob, sandpaper, your favorite blanket.

- Discuss the differences in texture.

- Repeat the activity with eyes closed and guess the item they are touching.

Discuss how blind people read Braille.

Gum Chewing Activity

- Gather a variety of flavors of sugar-free gum.

- Give each student a piece to hold in their hand, and have them try to guess the flavor.

- With their eyes closed, students rest the gum on their tongue.

- DO NOT CHEW IT!

- After a few seconds students may begin to slowly chew the gum.

- As they chew, ask them to see if they can identify the flavor of the gum.

- With younger students you may tell them what the possible flavors may be.

- This can also be done with chocolate, raisins, mints or other small treats.

Please see the Reference on page 107 for the exact url for articles, videos, and more.

Breathing Exercises Appendix: Mindful Breathing – Listening (page 124)

Circle a word, discuss, share, post, and add more.

GRADES 9 - 12

Creating a Personalized Mindfulness Practice

GOAL OF THIS SECTION: EMPOWER STUDENTS TO DEVELOP A PERSONAL PRACTICE THAT WILL HELP THEM SUCCESSFULLY MANAGE THE STRESSES OF DAILY LIFE.

Benefits of Mindfulness

Deep Breathing - Parasympathetic nervous system

"Rest and Digest"

The parasympathetic nervous system:

- Relaxes the body and inhibits or slows many high energy functions (the opposite of fight or flight)

- Lowers the heart rate and blood pressure

- Reduces anxiety levels

- Decreases adrenalin overload

- Lowers stress hormones

- Promotes digestion and the uptake of nutrients

- Improves ability to fall asleep, stay asleep, and reach a deeper REM sleep state

The **parasympathetic nervous system** is activated through **breathing exercises.**

Students will learn how to decrease anxiety and stress and increase feelings of calm and control using breathing skills. Developing these skills can help students manage test taking anxiety, performance anxiety (presentations, sports, theater), and social anxiety.

Video: Ten Incredible Benefits of Deep Breathing[71]

Mouth breathing only utilizes 10-20% of lung capacity. This shallow breathing uses the upper lungs and chest and prompts us to hyperventilate, alerting a fight or flight response.

Nose breathing stimulates the lower lung to distribute greater amounts of oxygen throughout the body signaling a calming response.

Nasal breathing is healthier than mouth breathing for several reasons: Exhaling through the nose, which is smaller than the mouth, creates greater air pressure and therefore a slower exhalation. This gives the lungs extra time to extract a greater amount of oxygen.

Gratitude

"A study was done with 9th and 10th grade students and found that students who expressed gratitude to parents, teachers, or coaches felt closer and more connected to them, which then increased their desire to improve themselves, as well as their confidence and competence in working toward this self-improvement."

- Greater Good Science Center, University of California, Riverside (2016)

People Who Practice Gratitude Consistently Experience:

- Stronger immune systems and lower blood pressure

- Higher levels of positive emotions

- More joy, optimism, and happiness

- Acting with more generosity and compassion

- Feeling less lonely and isolated

Activities

Neuroplasticity

Neuroplasticity is the ability of the brain to create behavior changes in response to mindfulness activities.

Students view Neuroplasticity Video by Sentis[38] to learn how to create new pathways in the brain to replace unwanted actions, thoughts and habits.

Teen Stressors

Mindfulness decreases the production of the stress hormone cortisol which increases the body's ability to manage stress and anxiety.

Mindfulness for Teen Anxiety: A Workbook for Overcoming Anxiety at Home, at School, and Everywhere Else by Christopher Willard[40]

Please see the Reference on page 107 for the exact url for articles, videos, and more.

<u>79th Organ</u> *(see activity on page 40)*

Testing your anxiety from <u>Growing Up Mindful</u> by Christopher Willard[72].

We have 78 organs, all of which we need to maintain health. To lose one causes pain. Our smart phones are our 79th organ.

<u>Exchange Phone</u>

- Have students look at their turned-off phone.

- Notice it. Notice emotions, urges, body response to it.

- Turn on the phone.

- Swap with a partner, then notice feelings.

- After a minute, tell students to switch back.

- Share and reflect what feelings occurred, what was felt? Why?

<u>Heartfulness</u>

Teacher should definitely be included!

- Each student in the class writes their name on a piece of paper.

- All of them are passed around so that each student can write a complimentary word for their classmates.

- Teacher can model by writing the first word for each student.

Mindful Minute

Releasing Fear

Teacher should instruct students to do the following:

- Breathe in calm.

- Breathe out worry.

- Breathe in peace.

- Breathe out fear.

Single Tasking

- Another way to describe mindfulness.

- Just do what you're doing, be aware of just that, nothing else.

- Breathe, notice only this.

Glitter Jar - "Settling Our Glitter"

- Watch glitter settle and compare to our thoughts.

- Use as a timer - 1-1/2 to 2 minutes. Then start class.

- Shake jar, breathe mindfully until glitter settles.

Visualization and Sound

For one minute think of favorite colors, places, beach scenes, friends, memories.

Meditation

Jade Meadow: A Guided Visualization Teens LOVE[20] (4:30 mins)

Nature. Beauty. Gratitude - Louie Schwartzberg[73] (5:17 mins)

Guided Meditation: Mindfulness of Emotion by Mindfulness Sanctuary[42] (10 mins)

Body Scan for Youth Athletes by Your Mindful Teen[75] (7 mins)

Mindfulness Teen: SOBER Breathing Space(Stop, Observe, Breathe, Expand & Respond)[21]

Three-Minute Breathing Space by Mindful[76]

Resources

Phil Jackson and Oprah: "How Phil Jackson Taught His Teams Mindfulness"[77]

"Mindfulness: Youth Voices" by KeltyMentalHealth[78]

Neuroplasticity and the Brain: "Neuroplasticity" by Sensis[38]

The Internet and the Brain: "What the Internet Is Doing to Our Brains"[79]

"Under Pressure - Mindfulness for Teens"[80]

Difference between Empathy and Sympathy: "Brené Brown on Empathy"[81]

Books

Mindfulness for Teen Anxiety: A Workbook for Overcoming Anxiety at Home, at School and Everywhere Else by Christopher Willard[40]

A Still Quiet Place for Teens: A Mindfulness Workbook to Ease Stress and Difficult Emotions by Amy Saltzman[41]

The Compassion Workbook for Teens by Karen Bluth, Ph.D[84]

Growing Up Mindful by Christopher Willard[72]

Make the Most of You by Patrick Lindsay[82]

The Mindful Athlete by George Mumford[83]

Please see the Reference on page 107 for the exact url for articles, videos, and more.

REFERENCE

When referring to the Reference section in print copy, type the "bit.ly" url (case sensitive) listed below into your browser to view the content.

1. Breathing with a Sphere by Elizabeth Miller
youtube.com/watch?v=1gKpdanmllA
     bit.ly/McLeanMSMC1

2. Poster, Mindfulness On-the-Go
docs.google.com/document/d/1_eP5CzJFi0N5c0Vlr5QEkEsrpjh7GoRIZ8e1qOCEysE/edit
     bit.ly/McLeanMSMC2

3. Calming Meditation Videos
Google "Calming Meditation" Videos
     bit.ly/McLeanMSMC3

4. Sesame Street Belly Breathing Activity with Elmo
youtube.com/watch?v=_mZbzDOpylA
     bit.ly/McLeanMSMC4

5. Reading of Puppy Mind by Andrew Nance
youtube.com/watch?v=Xd7Cr265zgc
     bit.ly/McLeanMSMC5

6. 4-7-8 Breathing Exercise by GoZen
youtube.com/watch?v=Uxbdx-SeOOo
     bit.ly/McLeanMSMC6

7. Breathing Sticks Video
drive.google.com/file/d/0B2Jn2qtna4k1VmJvOFlzSTJOeDQ/view
     bit.ly/McLeanMSMC7

8. "Yoga 4 Classrooms" Cards
yoga4classrooms.com/activity-card-deck
    bit.ly/McLeanMSMC8

9. Kids Relaxation Blog
kidsrelaxation.com
    bit.ly/McLeanMSMC9

10. Guided Meditations for Mindfulness Videos
Google "Guided Meditations for Mindfulness" Videos
    bit.ly/McLeanMSMC10

11. Don't Flip Yo' Lid Video By Fabian Jackson and Glenview Elementary, Madison, WI
youtube.com/watch?v=he-fW9_3egw
    bit.ly/McLeanMSMC11

12. Taming the Palace Guard one Breath at a Time by The Mindful Classroom
themindfulclassroom.wordpress.com/tag/amygdala/
    bit.ly/McLeanMSMC12

13. Calm Down and Release Amygdala
youtube.com/watch?v=Zs559gulGDo
    bit.ly/McLeanMSMC13

14. "Just Breathe" by Julie Bayer Salzman & Josh Salzman
youtube.com/watch?v=RVA2N6tX2cg
    bit.ly/McLeanMSMC14

15. Mindful Coloring Cover:
docs.google.com/document/d/12TmLFKvWDmpXiW_XaQwer7sNyDGuBSbG_vbiv7mOUs/view
    bit.ly/McLeanMSMC15

15b. Mindful Coloring Pages:
drive.google.com/file/d/0B2Jn2qtna4k1Rm9GdkVzQWVFQ0JDb3RCQmIwSFpfZ2s2ZVpB/view
    bit.ly/McLeanMSMC15B

16. "Release" Original Film on Middle School Anxiety by Mindful Schools
facebook.com/watch/?v=1271325922907729
    bit.ly/McLeanMSMC16

17. "NBA's Winningest Team Guided by Mindfulness and Joy" on mindful.org
mindful.org/nbas-winningest-team-guided-by-mindfulness-and-joy/
        bit.ly/McLeanMSMC17

18. "The Mindful Athlete with George Mumford - 10 minute Guided Meditation"
soundcloud.com/betterlisten/george-mumford-mindful-athlete-guided-meditation-10-minute
        bit.ly/McLeanMSMC18

19. "How NBA Coach Phil Jackson Taught His Players to Use Mindfulness"
youtube.com/watch?v=aqz7R-QalqY
        bit.ly/McLeanMSMC19

20. Jade Meadow: "A Guided Visualization Teens LOVE"
shantigeneration.com/wp-content/uploads/2013/03/03-jade-meadow.mp3
        bit.ly/McLeanMSMC20

21. Mindfulness Teen: "SOBER Breathing Space (Stop, Observe, Breathe, Expand & Respond)"
mindfulnessforteens.com/wp-content/uploads/2015/02/5.-SOBER-Breathing-Space.mp3
        bit.ly/McLeanMSMC21

22. "8 Hour Deep Sleeping Music: Delta Waves, Relaxing Music Sleep, Insomnia Music, Meditation"
youtube.com/watch?v=ScrrgEekpvw
        bit.ly/McLeanMSMC22

23. Dr. Daniel Siegel presenting a Hand Model of the Brain
youtube.com/watch?v=gm9CIJ74Oxw&t=1s
        bit.ly/McLeanMSMC23

24. Sesame Street: Bruno Mars: "Don't Give Up"
youtube.com/watch?v=pWp6kkz-pnQ
        bit.ly/McLeanMSMC24

25. Sesame Street: "Me Want It (But Me Wait)" - Impulse control with Cookie Monster
youtube.com/watch?v=9PnbKL3wuH4
        bit.ly/McLeanMSMC25

26. Sesame Street: "Feelings"
youtube.com/watch?v=BzDDmtw8L74
        bit.ly/McLeanMSMC26

27. Sesame Street: "Bert Gets Angry"
youtube.com/watch?v=zVLCXtG5HZ8
      bit.ly/McLeanMSMC27

28. "The Feelings Song"
youtube.com/watch?v=UsISd1AMNYU
      bit.ly/McLeanMSMC28

29. Feelings Song for Children by The Learning Station (Sad, Bad, Terrible Day)
youtube.com/watch?v=ca8SUuG8vdA
      bit.ly/McLeanMSMC29

30. Controlling Emotions: A Lesson from Angry Birds
youtube.com/watch?v=pFkRbUKy19g
      bit.ly/McLeanMSMC30

31. How Mindfulness Empowers Us: An Animation Narrated by Sharon Salzberg
vimeo.com/152432001
      bit.ly/McLeanMSMC31

32. The Struggle Switch - by Dr. Russ Harris
youtube.com/watch?v=rCp1l16GCXI&
      bit.ly/McLeanMSMC32

33. Wheel of Awareness by Dr. Daniel Siegel
drdansiegel.com/resources/wheel_of_awareness/
      http://bit.ly/McLeanMSMC33a

34. Marshmallow Test - Increase student understanding of impulse control
youtube.com/watch?v=QX_oy9614HQ
      bit.ly/McLeanMSMC34

35. Guided Meditations by Mindfulness for Teens
mindfulnessforteens.com/guided-meditations/
      bit.ly/McLeanMSMC35

36. Getting to Know and Love Your Brain Poster by Scholastic
drive.google.com/file/d/0B2Jn2qtna4k1VFhQQXhRbEEzdjlVY2w4ZzJLT0VfVmtaS2FR/view
      bit.ly/McLeanMSMC36

37. Gaia - Missing Links: Connections
facebook.com/Gaia/videos/vb.182073298490036/1428169147213772/?type=2&theater
        bit.ly/McLeanMSMC37

38. Neuroplasticity by Sentis
youtube.com/watch?v=ELpfYCZa87g
        bit.ly/McLeanMSMC38

39. Amygdala Hijack & Emotional Intelligence
youtube.com/watch?v=Lr-T6NAV5V4
        bit.ly/McLeanMSMC39

40. Mindfulness for Teen Anxiety: A Workbook for Overcoming Anxiety at Home, at School &
Everywhere Else
        Find me on Amazon: "Mindfulness for Teen Anxiety: A Workbook for Overcoming Anxiety at
        Home, at School, and Everywhere Else" by Christopher Willard PsyD
        bit.ly/McLeanMSMC40

41. A Still Quiet Place for Teens: A Mindfulness Workbook to Ease Stress and Difficult Emotions
        Find me on Amazon: "A Still Quiet Place for Teens: A Mindfulness Workbook to Ease Stress
        and Difficult Emotions" by Amy Saltzman MD
        bit.ly/McLeanMSMC41B

42. Mindfulness of Emotions Meditation
youtube.com/watch?v=h8kBXYj8kDg
        bit.ly/McLeanMSMC42

43. Sesame Street: Mark Ruffalo: Empathy
npr.org/sections/ed/2016/10/17/497827991/a-sesame-study-in-kindness
        bit.ly/McLeanMSMC43

44. "Have You Filled a Bucket Today?" by Carol McCloud
        Find me on Amazon: "Have You Filled a Bucket Today?: A Guide to Daily Happiness for Kids
        (Bucketfilling Books)" by Carol McCloud (Author), David Messing (Illustrator)
        bit.ly/McLeanMSMC44

45. "How to Fill Your Bucket" by Lisa Marie Performing Arts - Follow Up Lesson
youtube.com/watch?v=B4O7qIG3Fog
        bit.ly/McLeanMSMC45

46. The Gratitude Experiment Video
youtube.com/watch?v=U5lZBjWDR_c
        bit.ly/McLeanMSMC46

47. Gratitude Activity: 'Hunt the Good' to Find Happiness
docs.google.com/document/d/1-BC4h0CQKn_CrVhCIc3zD2exfcA6hUbuFu1xyGmneWM
        bit.ly/McLeanMSMC47

48. "How to Reduce Stress with Gratitude" Inspirational Reading by Nataly Kogan
docs.google.com/document/d/1BJGRYe7U2ul3lagzndB7hhc8-wQb3PaZ09eec3kb2uw
        bit.ly/McLeanMSMC48

49. Friendly Wishes by Annaka Harris - Guided Meditations
        static.nytimes.com/podcasts/2017/10/25/well/mindfulness-kid-wishes/96152920-annaka-
        harris-friendly-wishes-1.mp3
        bit.ly/McLeanMSMC49

50. GoZen! Loving-Kindness Meditation
youtube.com/watch?v=NC2aHvob0eo
        bit.ly/McLeanMSMC50

51. Gratitude Meditation (Strengthen Happiness) by Stop, Breathe & Think
youtube.com/watch?v=UhF8vLesRRc
        bit.ly/McLeanMSMC51

52. Skills to Overcome Self-Criticism & Embrace Who You Are by Karen Bluth
Find me on Amazon: Skills to Overcome Self-Criticism & Embrace Who You Are by Karen Bluth
        bit.ly/McLeanMSMC52

53. "Pooh's Little Instruction Book" by A.A. Milne
Find me on Amazon: "Pooh's Little Instruction Book" by A.A. Milne
        bit.ly/McLeanMSMC53

54. "Sick" by Shel Silverstein
poets.org/poetsorg/poem/sick
        bit.ly/McLeanMSMC54

55. Forest Hill South Park Gratitude Video
facebook.com/ForestHillSouthPark/videos/1290315797707803/
        bit.ly/McLeanMSMC55

56. Learning The Four Gates of Speech - The Indian Sufi Tradition
docs.google.com/document/d/1WpuqaD9H49oCn8Tpi2-msSshkx5QXLokK_K1wDvVl1k
        bit.ly/McLeanMSMC56

57. S.L.A.N.T. - Model, demonstrate, role play
docs.google.com/document/d/11_DBt4AXHa4l6P0GYMOYcb6n1opLSptPMNWv1CUPfPw
        bit.ly/McLeanMSMC57

58. T.H.I.N.K. - Steps to take before you speak
docs.google.com/document/d/1_BcnSP75_3fRvnSuEnx9Alf5GxW1M6mniwAAmN7MM7s
        bit.ly/McLeanMSMC58

59. Jaws Theme Song
youtube.com/watch?v=wCfWHqrYUqo
        bit.ly/McLeanMSMC59

60. Sad Violin
youtube.com/watch?v=-EQ6eHeBrhM
        bit.ly/McLeanMSMC60

61. The Angry Birds Movie - Main Orchestra Theme Music Video
youtube.com/watch?v=FN7905k0_kl
        bit.ly/McLeanMSMC61

62. Matoma - Wonderful Life (Mi Oh My)
youtube.com/watch?v=sm8zWsu-7mw
        bit.ly/McLeanMSMC62

63. Cheerful and Upbeat Music - Happy Background Music
youtube.com/watch?v=UNCmmK3vCQ8
        bit.ly/McLeanMSMC63

64. Katy Perry Firework - A Capella Cover - Mike Tompkins - Beatbox
youtube.com/watch?v=FyepYaE_JS4
        bit.ly/McLeanMSMC64

65. Blindfolded Fruit Tasting Game by Mindful Littles
mindfullittles.org/blindfolded-fruit-tasting-game/
        bit.ly/McLeanMSMC65

66. Sense of Taste & Smell - Our Tongue & Nose by MakeMeGenius
youtube.com/watch?v=j7GibFhuBmE
   bit.ly/McLeanMSMC66

67. How the Tongue Works by KidsHealth.org
youtube.com/watch?v=0hwOL91cjwM
   bit.ly/McLeanMSMC67

68. The Ice Cube Episode by Mindful Littles
mindfullittles.org/the-ice-cube-episode/
   bit.ly/McLeanMSMC68

69. How Your Skin Works by KidsHealth.org
youtube.com/watch?v=aMGgCxUyXT8
   bit.ly/McLeanMSMC69

70. "No Ordinary Apple" by Sara Marlowe
youtube.com/watch?v=CdN1xj6-2Mg
   bit.ly/McLeanMSMC70

71. Ten Incredible Benefits of Deep Breathing
youtube.com/watch?v=W4c6bg2fKg0
   bit.ly/McLeanMSMC71

72. Growing Up Mindful by Christopher Willard
   Find on Amazon: "Growing Up Mindful: Essential Practices to Help Children, Teens, and
   Families Find Balance, Calm, and Resilience" by Christopher Willard
   bit.ly/McLeanMSMC72

73. Nature. Beauty. Gratitude - Louie Schwartzberg
youtube.com/watch?v=gXDMoiEkyuQ
   bit.ly/McLeanMSMC73

74. Guided Meditation: Mindfulness of Emotion by Mindfulness Sanctuary
youtube.com/watch?v=h8kBXYj8kDg
   bit.ly/McLeanMSMC74

75. Body Scan for Youth Athletes by Your Mindful Teen
soundcloud.com/your_mindful_teen/body-scan-for-youth-athletes-meditation-only
   bit.ly/McLeanMSMC75

76. <u>Three-Minute Breathing Space by Mindful</u>
<u>youtube.com/watch?v=amX1IuYFv8A</u>
   <u>bit.ly/McLeanMSMC76</u>

77. <u>"How Phil Jackson Taught His Teams Mindfulness"</u>
<u>youtube.com/watch?v=aqz7R-QalqY</u>
   <u>bit.ly/McLeanMSMC77</u>

78. <u>"Mindfulness: Youth Voices" by KeltyMentalHealth</u>
<u>youtube.com/watch?v=kk7IBwuhXWM</u>
   <u>bit.ly/McLeanMSMC78</u>

79. <u>"What the Internet is Doing to Our Brains"</u>
<u>youtube.com/watch?v=cKaWJ72x1rl</u>
   <u>bit.ly/McLeanMSMC79</u>

80. <u>"Under Pressure - Mindfulness for Teens"</u>
<u>youtube.com/watch?v=hKnRKy5Wu7c</u>
   <u>bit.ly/McLeanMSMC80</u>

81. <u>"Brené Brown on Empathy"</u>
<u>youtube.com/watch?v=1Evwgu369Jw</u>
   <u>bit.ly/McLeanMSMC81</u>

82. <u>Make the Most of You by Patrick Lindsay</u>
<u>Find me on Amazon: Make the Most of You by Patrick Lindsay</u>
   <u>bit.ly/McLeanMSMC82</u>

83. <u>The Mindful Athlete by George Mumford</u>
<u>Find me on Amazon: The Mindful Athlete: Secrets to Pure Performance by George Mumford</u>
   <u>bit.ly/McLeanMSMC83</u>

84. <u>The Compassion Workbook for Teens by Karen Bluth, Ph.D</u>
<u>Find me on Amazon: The Compassion Workbook for Teens by Karen Bluth, Ph.D</u>
   <u>bit.ly/McLeanMSMC84</u>

Frankie Engelking

DIRECTOR OF STUDENT & COMMUNITY WELLNESS
McLEAN SCHOOL

Frankie Engelking began her work at McLean School over 20 years ago, bringing her expertise to students, faculty, and parents in her positions that include K-12 Health Education Coordinator, Middle School Dean of Students, Interim Head of the Middle School, and currently as the Director of Student and Community Wellness.

Ms. Engelking began her journey with Mindfulness in 2014 when she trained with Mindful Schools and began sharing the benefits of Mindfulness practice in schools with students, faculty, staff, and parents in the community. McLean's Mindfulness Program is nationally recognized as a leader in Mindfulness education and training. Ms. Engelking presented at the Northeast Regional Mindfulness Conference, Association of Independent Maryland Schools (AIMS), Association of Independent Schools of Greater Washington (AISGW) Head of School Conference, featured in an NBC4 news segment with anchor, Doreen Gentzler, on Student Learning and Mindfulness, and has contributed to articles in *The Atlantic*, *The Washington Post*, *Bethesda Magazine*, and *Science News for Students*.

Ms. Engelking's career began as a Patient Educator at the Washington Adventist Hospital in Takoma Park, Maryland and continued at the Area Health Education Center in Baltimore, Maryland as the Community Health Education Coordinator. After earning her Masters Degree in Education at The Catholic University of America, Ms. Engelking started a Health Education Consulting Company, working with over 22 schools in the Washington metropolitan area, providing Substance Abuse Prevention Training to County and State Government Agencies, and became a Certified Trainer for the Parent-to-Parent National Substance Abuse Prevention Program. For nine years she produced and hosted a live, call-in radio program, Perspectives on Health on WGTS 91.9 FM. She has appeared on the CBS This Morning show, participated in the production of several documentaries on the subject of Teen Behavior and Healthy Choices, and was a presenter at the National Association of Independent Schools (NAIS) National Conference in San Francisco.

Rosie Waugh

MINDFULNESS COORDINATOR
McLEAN SCHOOL

Rosie Waugh has over 30 years experience as an independent school educator. During that time she has served as a school administrator and classroom teacher. Ms. Waugh is the K-12 Mindfulness Coordinator at McLean School. Rosie received her formal training in Mindfulness through Mindful Schools and is a Certified Practitioner. Ms. Waugh has been part of a team of McLean School faculty and administrators who have implemented a school-wide K-12 Mindfulness Program for students, faculty, staff, and parents.

Her own Mindfulness journey began in 2014 when the practice was introduced to students and teachers by a McLean School parent. With the support of the Head of School, Michael Saxenian, Ms. Waugh organized training for over 30 teachers and staff. As her own personal practice began to evolve, she realized the importance in bringing Mindfulness to students and teachers in an honest and heartfelt way. Rosie is very passionate about the practice and continues to see the positive influence of Mindfulness on the McLean School community, inside and outside the classroom.

Frankie Engelking, MA

DIRECTOR OF STUDENT & COMMUNITY WELLNESS
FENGELKING@McLEANSCHOOL.ORG
301.299.8277

Rosie Waugh, MEd, MS

MINDFULNESS COORDINATOR
RWAUGH@McLEANSCHOOL.ORG
301.299.8277

BREATHING EXERCISES APPENDIX:

Mindful Breathing 1

Mlndful Breathing (Body Scan)

Ring Bell (pause)

Today we are going to take a trip around our body.

Let's get our "Mindful Bodies" on. (pause)

Feet flat on the floor, hands in your lap.

Let your body be very still. (pause)

Let your eyes close and without using your hands,

try to pay attention to how your feet feel with your mind.

(pause)

Now move your attention to (pause in between each one)

Your knees

Your legs

Where your body touches the chair

Your belly (take a mindful breath here)

Shoulders

Arms

Fingertips

Head

Put your fingers to your ears

(pause)

Notice how your body feels right now (pause)

Ring Bell

Mindful Breathing 2

MIndful Breathing

Ring bell (pause)

Let's get our Mindful Bodies on. (pause)

Feet flat on the floor, hands in your lap.

Close your eyes. (pause)

Take 3 slow, mindful breaths. (pause)

Try to notice where you feel the breath the most

in your body . . . your nose, chest . . . (pause)

Now take a few more mindful breaths. (pause)

As you breathe say to yourself "breathing in,

breathing out." Repeat this a few times. (pause)

Take a moment to notice how your body feels right

now. (pause)

Ring bell.

Mindful Breathing – Emotions

Emotions

Ring bell (pause)

Let's get our "Mindful Bodies" on. (pause)

Close your eyes; try to be still and quiet. (pause)

Let's take 3 mindful breaths together now. (pause)

Take a moment to notice how you are feeling.

(pause)

Try to notice what emotions(s) you are feeling.

(pause)

Are you happy? (pause) Are you sad? (pause)

Angry? (pause) Peaceful? (pause) Anxious?

Or perhaps you're not feeling any emotions now.

(pause)

Take 3 more mindful breaths; notice how you

feel now. (pause)

Ring bell

Mindful Breathing – Heartfulness

Heartfulness

Ring bell.

Let's get our "Mindful Bodies" on. (pause)

Close your eyes. Feet flat on the floor. (pause)

Raise your right hand, now take that hand

and place it over your heart. (pause)

Picture someone who you want to send kind

thoughts to...some who is living. (pause)

Keep picturing that person in your mind and say

these words out loud with me:

May you be healthy and strong. (pause)

May you be happy. (pause)

May you be peaceful. (pause)

For the next few seconds continue to let those

kind thoughts flow from your heart to theirs.

(pause)

Ring bell.

Mindful Breathing – Gratitude

Gratitude

Ring Bell (pause)

Let's get our Mindful Bodies on. (pause)

Let's take 3 mindful breaths together now. (pause)

With your eyes closed, think of three things you

are grateful for. (pause)

Now . . . imagine ALL of those things are

surrounding you right now. (pause)

Notice how that makes you feel. (pause)

There might be sad things that happened today

or things that make us angry. But there are

many things in our life that might make us feel

happy if we focus on them. (pause)

Throughout the day, try to notice the things

that make you happy, things you are grateful

for. Now take 3 mindful breaths. Notice how

you feel. (pause)

Ring bell.

Mindful Breathing – Listening

Listening

Let's get our "Mindful Bodies" on. (pause)

Feet on the floor, hands in your lap.

Close your eyes and open your ears. (pause)

Let your ears rest on any sound. (pause)

The sounds can be in this room, in the hall,

outside or even in your own body. (pause)

Notice how you are feeling right now. (pause)

Again, focus on the sounds in and around you.

(pause)

Can you hear yourself breathing? (pause)

Take 3 slow mindful breaths. (pause)

Ring bell.

Printed in the USA
CPSIA information can be obtained
at www.ICGtesting.com
LVHW070039091123
763461LV00047B/1107